The
Godly Superwoman

by
Linda Hanner

THE GODLY SUPERWOMAN:
HOW TO BE A PROVERBS 31 WOMAN AND STAY SANE

Published by: Heaven's Harvest Ministries
                9050 County Road 11
                Maple Plain, MN 55359
                612-972-3762

© 2000 Linda Hanner

All rights reserved. Except for brief passages used for review purposes, no part of this publication may be reproduced, stored in a retrieval system, or transmitted in any form or by any means, electronic, photocopying, recording, or otherwise, without the prior written permission of the author.

Bible verses are quoted from the New International Version (NIV) unless otherwise noted.

ISBN 0-9622669-5-7

Cover art by Linda Hanner

Page design and typesetting by Carol J. Frick

10 9 8 7 6 5 4 3 2 1   00 01 02 03 04 05 06

Contents

Chapter 1—Thinking Like an Efficiency Expert   5

Chapter 2—Motivating the Kids   13

Chapter 3—Getting Help from Husbands   25

Chapter 4—Accomplishing the Task Faster   29

Chapter 5—Accomplishing More Tasks at the Same Time   39

Chapter 6—Making the Task More Fun   53

Chapter 7—Staying Sane   61

Epilogue   69

Heaven's Harvest Ministries contact information   70

Other publications available through Heaven's
   Harvest Ministries   70

THE GODLY SUPERWOMAN

... being confident of this, that he who began a good work in you will carry it on to completion until the day of Christ Jesus.
—Philippians 1:6

Chapter 1

Thinking Like an Efficiency Expert

I'M AN EFFICIENCY EXPERT at heart. I first realized it when I read the book *Cheaper by the Dozen* as a sixth-grader. The story is about a family with twelve children. The father, Frank Gilbreth, applied the expertise he'd gained as a professional efficiency expert to keep his home running smoothly.

Mr. Gilbreth was instrumental in awakening the efficiency expert in me. In fact, throughout my first several years of motherhood, I became obsessed with the idea of getting more done in less time. Even with four small children underfoot, I managed to get lots done by working in short spurts.

I was a do-it-yourselfer who took it to extremes. When I sewed, I sewed everything from the kids' snowmobile suits to my husband's jeans and suits. When I got into gardening, I filled the freezer and pantry shelves with enough frozen and canned fruits and vegetables to get our family of six through the entire winter and spring. For a few years there were eight of us because we took in refugees from Vietnam.

A magazine personality quiz once scored me as having nearly three times the points needed to be classified a "Type A"—the label psychologists apply to those of us who seem to have been born with a sense of urgency and competitiveness often mixed with impatience and perfectionism.

More often than not, I'd work until I was exhausted. Yet no matter how much I did, I was unsatisfied. If I got tons done one day, I'd set higher goals for the next. I was often anxious and resentful. By the time I tucked the kids in for the night, I was so tense I had to clench my teeth to keep from screaming. I was what has been called a "hostile Type A."

Today I'm still unquestionably Type A, but am well along in the process of being transformed from a "hostile Type A" to a "happy Type A." The transformation began more than 20 years ago when I first invited Jesus into my heart and admitted that I was helpless to change myself. At that point, God began a "good work" in me (Philippians 1:4–6).

The transformation process has at times been painful, but I can testify to God's faithfulness in seeing the work He began in me "through to completion." I am so grateful that He loved me so much that He has hung onto me—even through two suicide attempts—and He brought me "out of the pit," placing me on firm ground (Psalm 40:2). My desire is to share the love, joy, and peace that God has given me as well as the practical tips that I've learned through 30 years of being a wife, mom, and entrepreneur.

I suspect that some of you can identify with the "hostile A" syndrome. Others of you are Type B by nature but feel caught up in the Type A lifestyle. Still others of you are happy being Type A. The truth is that whether you're an A or B, hostile or happy, it's hard to avoid living a Type A lifestyle—and it's often a challenge to stay sane in such a fast-paced world. Many of you are juggling work, family, church and community responsibilities. Even those who don't work outside the home are easily pulled deeply into the spiral of volunteerism—and find themselves just as busy as if they held paying jobs.

No matter what your personality, God can transform you into a woman who is "clothed with dignity and strength" (Proverbs 31:25). This book is meant as much more than a collection of practical tips. It is offered as a lifeline based on Biblical principles that can help you successfully negotiate the often frantic world of modern motherhood—and stay sane.

Keeping in mind that most moms are constantly on the run, I've designed this book in a pocket/purse size to be read during those snatches of time you spend waiting—in a dentist's office, during a child's swimming or music lessons, or in a restaurant. My prayer is that this guide will help you learn to manage your time and responsibilities less stressfully—and that God's transforming power will allow you to discover the "peace that passes all understanding" (Philippians 4:7) as you go about your daily tasks.

During daily devotions, I recently noted that in Proverbs 31 there is the perfect description of a wife and mom who is a "happy Type A" as well as an efficiency expert. The passage contains an inspiring list of all that can be accomplished by the "capable wife" who honors God. As the passage demonstrates, it is Biblical to plan ahead and to set goals, but because we're humans who live in an imperfect world, it's not realistic to expect things always to go smoothly. In any given day or week, many factors affect how much you are able to accomplish—your energy level, your kids' energy level, unexpected interruptions, and much more.

As long as you are somewhat functional, thinking like an efficiency expert (EE) will help. My personal EE philosophy involves a five-step task analysis. Every project from housework to shopping goes through the following mental checklist:

- ✓ How can I get the task done faster?
- ✓ How can I accomplish more than one task at the same time?
- ✓ How can I motivate my kids to help?
- ✓ How can I utilize my husband's energy to help?
- ✓ How can I make the task more enjoyable?

Thinking Like an Efficiency Expert

In upcoming chapters, I'll elaborate on these five areas, providing some specific examples to get you started. As you embrace the EE mindset, you'll find yourself becoming more and more creative in coming up with ideas to save time, conserve energy and preserve sanity.

THE GODLY SUPERWOMAN

Train a child in the way he should go,
and when he is old he will not turn from it.
—Proverbs 22:6

Chapter 2

Motivating the Kids

I DECIDED TO PUT this chapter early in the book because I'm afraid that many of you have already lost hope of getting cooperation from your children. I admit it can be a challenge, but it's not as difficult as you might think if you take the right approach. The key is to get inside their minds—think about what would motivate you if you were a child. We all need incentives for accomplishing what we do. Our careers offer us the reward of paychecks or promotions. We agree to do volunteer work because we believe in a cause. Housework gets done because we relish residing in clean, organized environments. But kids need different incentives. They aren't likely to care as much as we do about an overflowing garbage can or a floor covered with muddy footprints.

While it's important to instill in your children and teenagers a sense of responsibility through teaching and example, it can also be helpful to consider the following "kid motivators":

bribery *competition* *reward*

Here are some suggestions based on kid-motivating strategies that have worked for me:

Instill the idea of work before fun. Never miss an opportunity to get productive energy from your kids. Before embarking on a fun

Motivating the Kids

outing, present a list of tasks that absolutely must get done before leaving. Anticipating the adventure ahead, your kids will plunge into chores that would ordinarily involve endless prodding on your part and whining on theirs.

If your kids haven't been conditioned to know when you mean business, it might take a time or two of sticking to your word to get good results. When my kids were young, before we'd head for the beach or the shopping mall I'd announce that we would not leave until the house was picked up, the laundry was folded, and dinner was ready to go on the table when we returned. I would work alongside them supervising until all assigned tasks were complete. They knew the faster they got the work done, the sooner we'd be on our way. Sometimes they would even pitch in to help one another to speed things along. The earlier you start this approach, the better—and the more consistently you apply it, the more effective you will be in getting cooperation. Even preschoolers can do simple jobs like putting clothes and other items away or fetching things you need for a task.

Preteen and early teen years are more of a challenge. At that age, my kids had very little time to help me out during the week. However, each time they needed a ride to a practice or game or to a friend's home, I'd give them a small assignment before we'd leave the house—such as taking out the garbage or setting the table for dinner that night. Since they invariably were anxious to get going, they'd hustle to get the task done.

Assign tasks according to interests and abilities. I found that one of my preteen sons did a nice job of folding clothes, especially if he could do it while he was watching television. And my daughter was a great organizer of drawers and cupboards.

From time to time, it helps to reassign or rotate tasks among kids as they become bored or as their interests change.

Turn projects into fun competitive events. Think about the enormous amount of energy youngsters expend romping in the yard or playing sports. Imagine capturing some of that energy for your own purposes. When the motive is competition, kids move. My preschoolers balked at readying themselves for bed until I challenged them to have pajama races to see who could get ready the fastest—or toy races to see who could get the most toys picked up before a timer went off. An only child can compete against herself, striving to break previously attained records.

Offer small rewards. Nominal monetary rewards for specific tasks are often good motivators for your children. A pack of gum purchased by a youngster with money earned for dusting the living room is relished more than one purchased by you. Occasionally, small change worked well in motivating my kids to practice musical instruments. My youngest son once got very discouraged about a piano piece he was assigned to learn for an upcoming recital. He moped about it until I placed a row of nickels across the piano ledge and told him he could take one each time he played through the piece. By the time the nickels were gone, he knew the piece. One dollar was a small price to pay for the saved frustration.

Remind them of the benefits to them. My daughter wasn't keen on mowing the lawn until I reminded her it was a good way to catch a little sun to boost her tan for the upcoming prom. A son going through a growing spurt might be interested in baking a double batch of cookies knowing he can eat half the results.

Keep a sense of humor and make life at home fun. We had been down to two kids at home for a few years when one of our adult sons called to see if he could move back home from out of state. I was thrilled that he was coming. But neatness was not one of his strong points, and I knew that I'd likely soon be nagging him about picking up. I decided to hold a family meeting (a rarity in our house) a few days after he arrived home. Instead of turning the gathering into a lecture, I devised a lighthearted multiple choice quiz on household responsibilities. The quiz served as a friendly reminder of simple ways family members could help reduce my frustration over pet peeves. It made more of an impact than if I had continually nagged them about these issues. They took it in good humor and it did help keep them on track—at least for a few months anyway.

On the next few pages you'll find some of the questions from that family cooperation quiz.

1. If shoes are removed upon entering the house, they should be:
   a) placed neatly next to the wall by the door
   b) put in the closet on the shoe rack
   c) kicked into the middle of the room
   d) either a, b, or c depending on the circumstances
2. If you notice that someone else has left dishes around the house, shoes in the middle of the floor, or the toilet lid up, it's appropriate to:
   a) ignore it because it's not your responsibility if you didn't do it
   b) take the initiative to pick up the dishes, tidy the shoes, shut the lid
   c) laugh because you know Mom will be irritated, and it's kind of fun to see her face scrunch up and turn red
3. After cleaning the kitchen, dish cloths should be:
   a) wadded in a ball and left in the bottom of the sink
   b) left to soak all day in the unemptied dishpan
   c) rung out and hung neatly over the dishwasher handle

4. If you prepare a meal or snack, you should:

   a) leave the mess for the next person to clean up

   b) leave the kitchen as clean or cleaner than when you started

   c) leave all the food out with covers off because someone else might get hungry in the next few hours

5. The toilet lid should be left up:

   a) if the toilet is flushed

   b) if the toilet is not flushed

   c) only when in use

   d) never

6. Keeping the house clean and tidy is:

   a) Mom's job

   b) Dad's job

   c) Jenny and Mom's job

   d) Jason and Jonathan's job

   e) everyone's job

7. As a member of the family, you are responsible for helping to keep the house in order. An appropriate amount of time for each member to spend on household tasks each week is:
   a) 20 hours
   b) 8 hours
   c) 2 hours (less than 15 minutes a day)
   d) none

Write down specific instructions if you want chores done while you're away from home. I'd often assign chores for my preteens and teens while I was away from home and return to find them undone or only partially done. I discovered that writing a to-do list and reviewing it with them before I left greatly increased the probability of completion. The more specific the instructions, the better. For instance, rather than writing "clean up the kitchen," I'd write "wash, dry and put away the dishes and wipe off all the counter tops." Encouraging them to check off each task on the list once it was completed provided additional motivation.

Be alert for opportunities. If your ravenous teenagers are constantly hanging out in the kitchen, put them to work stirring, chopping, and organizing. When they are plunked in front of the television, put the children to work. By age 11 or 12, my daughter was a seasoned drawer organizer. Whenever I'd catch her in front of the television, I'd bring her some sorting projects to work on while she watched.

THE GODLY SUPERWOMAN

A wife of noble character who can find? She is worth far more than rubies. Her husband has full confidence in her . . . .
—Proverbs 31:10–11

Chapter 3

Getting Help from Husbands

THIS IS GOING TO BE a very short chapter since getting my husband involved in domestic affairs is the area in which I've had the least success. Some of you have husbands who don't mind housework or perhaps enjoy cooking. Mine has never shown such inclinations. Don't get me wrong. He's a great guy who works hard, loves his family and has stood by me through thick and thin. But he considers it my job to do the cooking, cleaning and laundry. Perhaps his lack of interest in these chores goes back to the dynamics of our relationship as 19-year-old newlyweds. Determined to be the quintessential wife, I'd get up at 5:00 AM to make him breakfast before we both left for work, and race home to see that dinner was ready for him soon after he arrived home. On the other hand, he was determined to prove himself macho by not succumbing to traditional "women's work."

Eventually I stopped trying to be perfect, but found it's not easy for men to change established behavior patterns. We've made some headway though. After many years of me doing all the grocery shopping (one of my least favorite tasks), we turned Friday evenings into a combined family outing and grocery shopping trip. We'd pile the kids into our compact station wagon, eat at a restaurant and do something fun like mini-golf. Then we'd wrap up the evening by team grocery shopping. Everyone helped gather and bag groceries at the store and unload them when we got home.

Getting Help from Husbands

If your husband is a TV watcher like mine, utilize his muscle power for mindless tasks that won't interfere with his program, such as mixing cookie dough or pie crust, or cutting vegetables.

According to Carol, a good friend of mine, you can appeal to some men through their love of gadgetry. She has noticed that bread machines are very popular with many men who wouldn't consider making bread (or anything else) the old-fashioned way. The latest in high-tech vacuum cleaners or a food chopper with 87 accessories can have irresistible appeal to a gadget-minded man.

If you haven't yet had much success in getting your husband involved in household tasks, don't give up hope. After 30 years of marriage to a husband who had never cooked anything other than frozen pizzas and canned tomato soup, I did once get him to stick around the kitchen long enough to help me bake an apple pie.

THE GODLY SUPERWOMAN

She sets about her work vigorously; her arms are strong for her tasks.
—Proverbs 31:17

Chapter 4

Accomplishing the Task Faster

AS A SELF-EMPLOYED person for most of my adult life, I am keenly aware that in business, time is money. It didn't take me long to learn that the faster I worked, the more I got done and the more money I made per hour. Another benefit to getting tasks done faster is that you have more time for other things.

On the next few pages, I offer some speed motivators that have gained me a great many precious hours over the years.

Eliminate steps. If it doesn't need doing, don't do it—like peeling potatoes for instance. I rarely do that anymore. I just scrub them, then slice them for frying, quarter them for pot roasts, or simply poke them with a fork and pop them in the microwave. Even potato salad and mashed potatoes made with unpeeled potatoes are acceptable these days.

Look for shortcuts. As a seamstress with four young children, I learned lots of tricks to speed up my work. I found it worked well to use weights rather than pins to hold patterns against fabric when cutting (anything in the vicinity worked—soup cans, knick-knacks, children's shoes). Eliminating pinning time easily reduced overall cutting time of a garment to less than half. And I no longer had to worry about toddlers finding stray pins.

Give yourself incentives on blah days. Moving sluggishly? Not getting much done? Clutter strewn around the house? Being home all day with young children can do that to you. Get yourself motivated by inviting a friend over for coffee in an hour, or promising the kids you'll go for a walk when the house gets picked up. When I lived in a neighborhood with several work-at-home moms, I found this change of pace would often lighten my mood and motivate me to get a lot done in a very short time.

Tackle the task as soon as possible. Depending on the task, you can often cut down on time and save energy by simply tackling it as soon as possible. This is true when it comes to soiled pots and pans. Soak them while you're eating dinner and they will be easy to clean immediately afterward. This concept is also true when it comes to keeping the garden weeded. Most weeds are much easier to knock out with a hoe before their roots are embedded deeply in the soil. Tackling a problem when it's small keeps it from getting bigger and more difficult to handle.

Consider the location. Working outdoors is often a great way to save on cleanup time. On nice summer days, I almost always fed my young children and their friends lunch and snacks outside. This made for easy cleanup. A large cake pan or mixing bowl made a better carryall than a tray from which items could easily topple. I used one cake pan for plates, cups and utensils and another for sandwich fixings, veggies, and fruit. I'd simply throw everything into the cake pan, grab a cutting board, and hand one of the kids a pitcher of milk or juice to carry. I'd put the sandwiches together and cut up the fruit outside. If you don't have a deck or picnic table, kids don't mind just sitting on the steps or on a blanket spread on the grass. After lunch, there are no counters to wipe. You can place the dishes and utensils back in the cake pan, add a little dish soap and rinse thoroughly with the garden hose. We even had the advantage of goats and chickens as handy, outdoor garbage disposals!

Lots of other projects can be done outdoors. When I was very involved in sewing, I'd place a large cutting board on top of the picnic table to do my garment cutting there. This saved the hassle of vacuuming fabric threads and lint from carpeting. When I had fresh garden vegetables such as string beans to prepare for cooking, I'd sit on a lawn chair with a pan of ice water on one side and a container of beans on the other. I'd break the ends, snap them into bite-size pieces, then drop them into the ice water to keep fresh until I brought them back in the house. I liked getting a little sun as I worked, but others might prefer to park their lawn chairs in the shade.

Time yourself. When my kids were small, my energy often waned by the end of the day. I was not in the mood to stay in the kitchen to clean up after dinner. But when I started timing myself, I found it easier to stay on track. Focusing on working quickly, I discovered the job could be accomplished in 15 minutes or less. When I realized how little time it took when I put my mind to hustling, it no longer seemed daunting.

Get rid of excess clutter. Are you a victim of the "someday factor"? That's what my aunt, Agnes Brown, called it in her book, *Cathartic Confessions of a Stockpiler*. Here are a few of the excuses she describes for stockpiling:

What if I need it . . . someday.

I might use it . . . someday.

It might be worth something . . . someday.

I will fix it . . . someday.

I might find a new part . . . someday

My kids might use it . . . someday.

I might find the mate . . . someday.

It will *come back in style* . . . *someday.*
I will *lose weight* . . . *someday.*
I *might gain weight* . . . *someday.*
I *can make something out of it* . . . *someday.*
I *will have it when I need one* . . . *someday.*
I *can use it for dirty jobs* . . . *someday.*
I *can use it for parts* . . . *someday.*
I *can put things in it* . . . *someday.*
It *might start working again* . . .*someday.*
I *will have a garage sale* . . . *someday.*

Aunt Agnes points out that 99.9 percent of the time "someday" doesn't come. Since one can generally work a lot faster without excess clutter, it is often best to part with it. It also feels defeating to have lots of uncompleted projects around. Occasionally, I start a craft project and get stuck on it. After a year of moving it from one place to another, I finally donate it to charity along with instructions for completion. Someone else might be more motivated to pick up where I've left off. I'm then more inspired to start a new project that I'm more likely to complete.

Turn on some lively music. When I find myself plodding through morning tasks at a snail's pace feeling absolutely no motivation, I put on a favorite tape or CD. As I sing along, my pace soon starts picking up to match the beat of the music. I find praise and worship music to be the most effective at lifting my mood and pace. Many passages of Scripture affirm that praising God through song draws one closer to Him while sending demons fleeing. It's a given that you'll work faster without being harassed by "spirits" of apathy, depression, or lethargy.

Accomplishing the Task Faster

Take joy in your ability to work. Sometimes seeing things from a different perspective can help ward off the temptation to procrastinate. Many of us have discovered that one of the most frustrating aspects of being ill for an extended time or recovering from injury is being unable to do for ourselves the ordinary chores that we otherwise do without thinking, or maybe even complain about. Running up and down stairs to the laundry room, driving to the grocery store, mowing the lawn—after weeks or months in bed, in a wheelchair, or on crutches, these begin to seem like treasured privileges rather than annoying chores. It can return the sparkle to our efforts if we keep in mind that health and strength—and our ability to work—are gifts that should not be taken for granted.

THE GODLY SUPERWOMAN

She watches over the affairs of her household and does not eat the bread of idleness.
—Proverbs 31:27

Chapter 5

Accomplishing More Tasks at the Same Time

IN PREPARING to present my first Superwoman workshop, I decided to check out what the national experts had to say on efficiency. There are a number of popular books on juggling work and family and running a household efficiently. Some advise organizational regimens that I know I'd never follow—like keeping rotating note-card files. Others advise campaigning for family-friendly changes in the workplace or provide specific housekeeping tips such as 1,001 ways to use baking soda. Most are written by women, but the expert with whom I best identify is a man named Don Aslett. This nationally known housecleaning expert thinks like I do. I suspect that he too was born an EE. In his books, he bases his housekeeping tips on some good principles. One I've applied in many situations is what he calls the "multiple-track system." Don applies this concept to housework; I use it in lots of other situations. The key, as he says, is to use your time productively—don't wait until one task is done before starting another. Here's an example of how I might apply Don's multi-track system while getting ready for work:

> I get out of bed at 5:50 AM and head for the laundry room to start a load of laundry, then on to the kitchen to take chicken breasts from the freezer. As the washing machine gets going, I put a cup of water to heat in the microwave and take 10 minutes for morning devotions. Then

Accomplishing More Tasks at the Same Time

I shower, dry my hair (getting in a few leg stretching exercises and drinking a cup of coffee). By the time my hair is dry and my makeup is on, the washing machine has completed its cycle. I put the clothes in the dryer and return to the kitchen to cut up the partially thawed chicken breasts and chop an assortment of fresh vegetables (takes just about 10 minutes). The chicken and vegetables go in the refrigerator to be used for stir-fry at dinnertime. Back to the clothes dryer, I remove the now fluffy blouses and shirts and put them on hangers to save ironing time, and turn the dryer back on to finish drying socks, underwear and towels. By 6:50 I've finished dressing, placed the dry laundry in a basket (to fold later) and am ready to head for work. When I return from work it will take less than 15 minutes to cook a pot of rice and stir-fry the chicken and vegetables for dinner. (I plan even further ahead and cook enough of the chicken to add to a pasta dish the following evening.) The socks, underwear and towels can be folded while catching a few minutes of evening news. (If teens or a willing husband *arrive home before you, I'd suggest leaving instructions for them to finish the stir fry and fold the laundry before you get home.)*

I must admit that I don't always function efficiently enough to keep a complex multi-track system going. But I do try to accomplish more than one task simultaneously whenever possible and there are lots of ways to do so. Here are just a few:

In the kitchen—

Cook several meals simultaneously. I often cook two or three meals at once. This reduces energy and time spent on preparation, monitoring, and cleanup per meal. As an example, a goulash casserole, sloppy joes, and chili can easily be prepared simultaneously. I start by browning three pounds of ground beef with chopped onions. Meanwhile, I get noodles boiling. Once the beef is browned, I put two-thirds of it in a microwaveable bowl, then add the other casserole ingredients and noodles to the pound of ground beef still in the pan. The casserole then goes to the oven to finish cooking (usually to serve that night). The empty noodle pan (no need to wash it) is then used for combining one pound of the remaining cooked ground beef with the chili ingredients. While the chili is simmering, I add sloppy joe ingredients to the remaining pound of browned beef. The sloppy joe mixture can be microwaved on low for 15 minutes or placed in the refrigerator. While the casserole is cooking, I prepare the salad and set the table for that evening's meal.

After dinner, the sloppy joes and chili are ready to cool and refrigerate for a meal the next day or later in the week. I have just two pans to wash, and the next two meals will involve almost no preparation and only minimal cleanup. The sloppy joes and chili can be reheated in the microwave. Since each of these meals keeps well for several days in the refrigerator (chili is much tastier reheated), I can serve them on alternate days to avoid having meals based on ground beef three days in a row. Here are these three-in-one recipes:

BASIC BROWNED GROUND BEEF MIXTURE

Brown 3 to 5 pounds of ground beef, adding chopped onion and celery to taste. Divide into thirds and add ingredients as follows:

GOULASH

Add the following to browned ground beef mixture and bake about 30 minutes at 350 degrees:

1 large can (28 oz.) tomatoes	1 can (10 3/4 oz.) tomato soup
1 teaspoon salt	1/8 teaspoon pepper
1 1/2 teaspoon cumin	1 small can mushrooms (optional)

6 cups cooked egg noodles or elbow macaroni

Accomplishing More Tasks at the Same Time

CHILI

Add the following to browned ground beef mixture and simmer 30 minutes or more:

1 can (16 oz.) chili beans	1 large can (28 oz.) tomatoes
1 teaspoon salt	1/8 teaspoon pepper

chili powder to taste (I use about 1 tablespoon)

SLOPPY JOES

Add the following to the browned ground beef mixture and simmer about 20 minutes:

1 cup catsup	1/2 cup water
1 teaspoon salt	1/8 teaspoon pepper
1/2 teaspoon vinegar	1 teaspoon prepared mustard
1 tablespoon brown sugar	1/2 teaspoon lemon juice

2 teaspoons Worcestershire sauce

Cook in quantity. When I don't prepare several different meals at once, I usually cook at least twice the amount needed for one meal. I then divide it into meal-size quantities. Some can be refrigerated or frozen for later use.

At times I disguise leftovers so my family thinks they are getting two different meals. For instance, I prepare an extra-large roast adding lots of vegetables. After dinner, I cut up the leftover meat and veggies into stew-size pieces and add them to the remaining gravy, and it becomes instant stew to serve with fresh buns or biscuits a few days later.

Catch up on phone calls while preparing meals. Just before dinner, when you need to hang around the kitchen to keep food from burning, is a good time to catch people at home and works especially well if you are calling to leave brief messages. It is likely to minimize time spent on the phone, since most people you call are likely to be getting ready for dinner too, and will not want to spend a lot of time chatting. When I save calls until later in the evening I spend more time talking—time that would be better spent with family or working on other projects.

Purchase a full year's supply of greeting cards at one time. This will save you lots of stops and could save hours of waiting in line over the course of a year. If you live near a warehouse that sells cards at a discount, all the better. Pick up a few extra wedding, sympathy and get-well cards. Sympathy cards especially are good to have on hand. One woman I know says she purchases cards for the year and addresses them right away so they are ready to send at appropriate times.

In the car—

Read junk mail while riding in the car. My time at home is precious and I'd rather not spend it sorting through non-urgent mail. I keep a folder handy for this type of mail and bring it along to sort and review while riding in the car. Since we live 30 minutes or more from most relatives and from shopping malls, this helps pass the time. When we arrive at our destination, I can simply throw what I don't need to save into the nearest trash receptacle. If you recycle, have a sack ready for stashing recyclable junk mail.

Tone up while waiting at stoplights or on ramps. Doing isometric exercises while waiting at stoplights or ramps keeps me from getting too impatient (or falling asleep), while helping me stay in shape. I do thigh tighteners, arm presses, and have even devised some eye-muscle exercises to help keep the skin under my eyes from sagging.

Accomplishing More Tasks at the Same Time

Memorize speeches. Driving time is a good time to memorize speeches. I outline speeches, record them and listen to them on my way to and from work or appointments—and one last time on my way to actually give the talk. By the time I've listened to it three or four times, I usually know it well enough to present it reasonably smoothly.

While 49housework—

Learn something new. As many women do, I started college several years after I was married and had started raising kids. With family, housework, and a job, my study time was limited. I resolved some of the problem by reading all my lecture notes onto audiotape to listen to while doing housework. Taping the notes and listening to them was often more efficient than listening to the actual lecture. It made a more concise tape and the process of reading the notes aloud also helped reinforce the information. Even though I wasn't usually fully attuned to the tapes, by the time I had played them several times, I knew the information well enough to ace the tests.

Get a workout. Put some energy into your housework. Work to fast-paced music. You can do deep knee bends while folding clothes, arm stretches while reaching for cobwebs, leg exercises while marching up and down stairs (tighten your thighs as you go) to put things away. I might start out the day feeling tired and unmotivated, but taking this approach almost invariably puts me in a more energetic mode.

While waiting for appointments—

Waiting in the doctor's or dentist's office can be nerve-wracking. I always come prepared just in case they're behind schedule. My work packet is supplied with hand-sewing projects and paper for note and letter writing. Near the holiday season, I might bring Christmas cards to address.

While on the telephone—

Consider keeping small mindless projects in convenient locations to work on when talking on the phone—like hand mending and sewing on buttons. With the modern convenience of portable phones (and headsets), I find I can do just about any relatively quiet household task while talking, such as washing floors, cleaning closets, and dusting.

THE GODLY SUPERWOMAN

She is clothed with strength and dignity;
she can laugh at the days to come
—Proverbs 31:28

Chapter 6

Making the Task More Fun

DO YOU DREAD certain tasks, yet find it bothers you even more if they aren't done? I feel that way when it comes to dusting and laundry. Although dusting is a pain, I am uncomfortable in a dusty house, and regardless of my aversion to the tediousness of folding clothes, the task needs to get done. In these cases, I look for ways to make the job more pleasant. For this chapter I've gathered some of my favorite strategies for taking the tedium out of chores. Try some and you'll soon be inventing your own.

Tackle the unpleasant tasks in a pleasant environment. I love being outdoors. In fact, I get downright irritable in nice weather when I can't get out of the house for a few hours. So I do as much as I can outside. Next time you have towels to fold, buttons to sew on, silver to polish, or paperwork to catch up on, and the weather is beautiful, consider taking your work outdoors. Even tedious research can be less boring when done from a lawn chair with a light breeze brushing one's skin. I've gotten some of my best tans while sewing or folding clothes by our picnic table. When I had preschoolers, working outdoors provided an added advantage because I could supervise them as they played. An ice cooler with treats for the kids cut down on treks through the house. A plastic bucket with a washcloth and towel outside the door allowed for a quick sticky-kid wash—first faces, then hands, and finally feet—before we all came back inside.

Making the Task More Fun

Distract yourself mentally. Check the library for interesting audiotapes and absorb some useful information while getting chores done. Breeze through boring tasks while listening to a favorite radio program. Or you might prefer working to pleasant or peppy music.

Job-share. Working with a friend can make most chores almost painless. Consider talking to a friendly neighbor about work-lightening strategies. For instance, if you have an aversion to washing floors and she dreads laundry, perhaps it would benefit you to trade a task for a task. Or how about forming a meal cooperative with a few other nearby families. Each couple could cook for three families one night, then have two evenings free from kitchen duty. It doesn't take much longer to prepare single-dish meals like chili, lasagna, soup or casserole for three families than it does for one. The couple assigned the cooking can also deliver the meals to the other homes. (When making such agreements, it might be best to do so on a short-term trial basis to start.)

For big events like graduation parties, I joined forces with a few neighbors. We helped each other prepare all the food, which took much of the stress out of planning and preparation.

Focus on the end results. My mother-in-law once asked, "Don't you ever have a day when you don't feel like doing anything?" To be honest, I do have days when I'm not the least bit motivated. On those days, I tell myself that even though I don't give a rip today, tomorrow I'll likely be glad for whatever I've accomplished today. I start with a goal to get just one or two small tasks done. Once I get started, it becomes easier to keep going.

Recognize side benefits. When you concentrate on the benefits of your labor rather than the labor itself, you'll find a new appreciation for it. With a laundry room in the basement and bedrooms upstairs, I whined about continually running up and down stairs until I focused on the good workout I was getting without the time and expense of joining a health club.

Think about the importance of the task. When it came to kid care, I found my attitude improved immensely when I thought about what it would be like if I couldn't be there for them when they woke up needing my attention at night. I soon found myself thanking God that I was there to care for and comfort them. Being there for my children, even in the middle of the night, became an acknowledged blessing.

Make it a race against time. Earlier I mentioned timing tasks to get them done faster, but it also seems less like drudgery when you turn chores into a game by racing against time to see how fast you can get them done. No task that can be scrunched into 15 minutes or less can be terribly depressing. I can fold a load of clothes in five minutes if I put my mind to it. I can dust just about any room in less than 10 minutes, and de-cobweb every room in the entire house within 15 minutes if my goal is to set a new speed record as I'm doing it.

Alternate distasteful tasks with more pleasant tasks. To reduce the monotony of tedious tasks like folding clothes, I sandwich folding laundry between tasks that I find more pleasant—like organizing cupboards.

If you don't like to do it and it's not necessary, don't do it. I read of a stay-at-home mom who burned herself out trying to be the perfect homemaker. One day she completely switched gears, abandoning homemaking for a full-fledged political career. Her family fell apart. Maybe she and her family would have suffered less in the long run if she had not worn herself to a frazzle cooking gourmet dinners and baking three-tiered cakes for every birthday celebration. I, too, once felt obligated to attempt lavish birthday cakes (although mine usually came out lopsided and not very artistic). After hours in the kitchen tracking through spilled flour and sticky frosting, I'd be hot, sweaty, and irritable. I finally stopped doing it. The few extra dollars spent on purchasing a cake were well worth the sanity gained. I stopped dreading birthdays and my children much preferred the Dairy Queen ice cream cakes over mine anyway.

For God hath not given us the spirit of fear, but of power, and of love, and of a sound mind.
—2 Timothy 1:7 (KJV)

Chapter 7

Staying Sane

I DID NOT DECIDE to write this book because I think of myself as the ideal homemaker, or because I've always been sane. In fact, as a young mom I struggled with depression and experienced a mental breakdown that resulted in a 12-day hospital stay. In addition, for six years I dealt with a physical illness and at one point was put on a medication that plunged me into a psychosis.

Although I would never choose to relive the pain of those experiences, I'm not sorry for them. God strengthened me through them, and I learned valuable lessons. Many women who are familiar with my earlier struggles have shared their own often well-concealed struggles with depression and anxiety. They find inspiration in knowing that someone who experienced extreme lows can be brought out of the "pit" to once again function well in a tumultuous world.

I pray that if you should happen to buckle, whether it be due to intense demands or hormonal imbalance or any other circumstance, that you won't lose hope. With God's help, you can come through stronger, just as I did. For me, it meant learning to release my circumstances to God, and to accept graciously the love and prayers of others even though they couldn't really understand what I was going through.

Here are what I see as important keys to maintaining sanity and order in one's life:

Staying Sane

Be realistic. As Don Aslett says, "Even in the cartoon world, Wonder Woman in all her glory never raised children, stabilized a husband, or cleaned and managed a house. Wonder Woman only faced criminals, not housework horrors." No one can do everything and none of us feels in control all of the time. When you start to feel overwhelmed, allow yourself as much leeway as you can. Often just letting go of a few tasks helps. A few canceled meetings might be all it takes to relieve a sense of growing panic. An evening off and a good night's sleep can do wonders for one's mental state.

Don't compare yourself to others. God made some of you organizers; others of you have been blessed with such creative minds that it's difficult to focus on a single task for any length of time. Some of you are energetic and like being on the move; others relish the thought of curling up on the couch for an entire afternoon with good book. When you learn to appreciate your uniqueness, you'll appreciate others as well. Our differences can make knowing each other more fun, and might help to give us balance. When you try to live up to perceived expectations of those around you, you'll never achieve them, because you'll try to match the strong points of everyone you meet (never taking into account differences in our energy levels and abilities).

I once lived next door to a woman who described her home as a "pig sty" during times that it looked to me like a candidate for a feature in *Better Homes and Gardens*. I was awed by it, and for a time I determined to emulate her style. I took inventory of her array of cleaning products. I purchased the floor shiners, the spray cleaner that made it possible for her refrigerator to double as a full-length mirror and the paste wax that kept her wood furniture so sleek the candy dishes nearly glided onto the floor.

But the harder I tried to be like her, the more tense and grouchy I became. I didn't take into account that I had a home business and that I enjoyed saving money by making my family's clothing. I really wasn't willing to give up these and other activities in exchange for a magazine-perfect home.

Focus on what you've accomplished. It's easy to get hung up on things that aren't done, rather than enjoying what has been accomplished. Keep a to-do list. Revel in what does get crossed off, not what doesn't, even if only a few items do. Dealing with a prolonged illness helped change my perspective in this regard. I learned to greatly appreciate even small accomplishments, like being able to help my kids practice spelling, or getting a few notes written to long-neglected friends.

Stop feeling guilty about saying no. Don't say yes to every volunteer opportunity just because someone insists you're the right person for the job and that the project will most certainly crash and burn without you. Amazingly, when illness forced me to relinquish my dozen or so volunteer roles, the world continued to revolve. My church remained functional, and the Parent-Teacher Organization flourished. Knowing that life goes on without you doesn't mean your contributions aren't valuable. Our energy levels vary at different times, and sometimes we simply need to allow others to carry us along a bit.

Take care of yourself. During my illness, I learned the importance of taking care of myself in order to be available to take care of others. Eat your fruits and vegetables, take stress-formula vitamins during times of extra stress, and get proper sleep as often as you can. Even so, there may be times when you can't do all that you want or need to do. I learned that accepting help from others can also be a way of giving, since people feel rewarded when they know they have helped where there is real need.

Start out your day as serenely as possible. If you start your day in a frenzy, you're likely to feel frenzied all day. At first I had to discipline myself to spend time in prayer and Scripture reading in the morning, but after doing it for several months it became a joy rather than a discipline. What started as a few minutes a day evolved into an hour or more, yet that time never really seems to cut into my day. When I take time to pray and allow God to speak to me through His Word, I find that I work more efficiently, am less anxious over disruptions, and can get along on less sleep.

Value your role. Don't underestimate your worth as a mother and homemaker. You may feel you're just fumbling along and the roles may seem thankless at times, but speaking from the perspective of a mom with four adult children, I'm being greatly rewarded for persevering. I've received considerable career-related praise in recent years, but that satisfaction pales compared to joy over positive feedback from my sons and daughter. I was far from a model parent. Yet, my kids affirm that my just being there to discipline, encourage, and instill Biblical values was vital. Today my kids have great respect for me—and our two "prodigal" sons have come back to the Lord after 10 years, proving Proverbs 22:6, which says that if we train our children in the way they should go, they will not turn from it.

Epilogue

SO MUCH HAS happened in my life since I started working on this book. Two of our children are now married and we have two grandchildren. My career has taken many turns, and a year ago God called me to start Heaven's Harvest Ministries. Our mission is to rally churches and individuals to work in harmony to advance God's kingdom here on earth. As I move forward, I'm learning to let God direct my steps and to tap into the awesome power He has made available to us as Christians.

I pray also that the eyes of your hearts may be enlightened in order that you may know the hope to which He has called you, the riches of His glorious inheritance in the saints, and His incomparably great power for us who believe.—Ephesians 1:18–20

Heaven's Harvest Ministries

If you are interested in learning more about Heaven's Harvest Ministries, write to: Linda Hanner
9050 County Road 11
Maple Plain, MN 55350

Other resources available through Heaven's Harvest Ministries:

Are There Tree Shrews in Your Family Tree? by Linda Hanner
In this 34-page easy-to-read overview of the facts about evolution, you'll discover why more and more people, including scientists, are turning away from evolution to embrace creation. A great resource for home-schoolers and discussion

groups. Single copy—$2.50. Six or more copies—$2.00 each. For mail orders, include $2.00 shipping and handling for 1–6 copies plus 50 cents for each additional 6 copies. Minnesota residents add 6.5% sales tax.

FaithSearch by Dr. Don Bierle with Linda Hanner—Geared for teens, this study guide was inspired by scientist Don Bierle's well-known book, *Surprised by Faith.* Based on evidence, it addresses the questions most frequently asked by young people: Why do I exist? Is God real? Is the Bible true? and Can I know God? Single copy—$9.00. Six or more copies—$8.00 each. For mail orders, include $3.00 shipping and handling per 1–6 books plus 50 cents for each additional book. Minnesota residents add 6.5% sales tax.

Healing Wounded Doctor-Patient Relationships by Linda Hanner with key contributions by John Witek, M.D. Based on Linda Hanner's extensive research, this book reveals the views both of doctors and of their patients regarding what is good and bad about the modern doctor-patient relationship, and it gives simple steps that doctors and patients can take to significantly improve the way they communicate and work together. Single copy—$14.95. For mail orders, include $3.00 shipping and handling for 1–6 books plus 50 cents for each additional book. Minnesota residents add 6.5% sales tax.

Of Power & Love & Sound Mind by Linda Hanner. The story of how the author's busy life was interrupted by the sudden onset of a devastating illness and her six-year search for a diagnosis for what turned out to be Lyme disease. As grateful as she was to finally be cured, learning to trust God and have faith in His plan for her life—even when no answers to the mystery of her illness were yet in sight—was the greater gift. Single copy—$12.95. For mail orders, include $3.00 shipping and handling per 1–6 books plus 50 cents for each additional book. Minnesota residents add 6.5% sales tax.